PAINTING OVER
THE GROWTH CHART

PAINTING OVER THE GROWTH CHART

poems

DAN RATTELLE

WISEBLOOD BOOKS

2024

WISEBLOOD BOOKS
P.O. Box 870
Menomonee Falls, Wisconsin 53052

Cover design by Amanda Brown
Photograph by Joakim Nådell
Typesetting by Louis Maltese

Printed in the United States of America
ISBN: 978-1-963319-93-4

I

II

And yet they think that their houses shall continue for ever, and that their dwelling-places shall endure from one generation to another; and call the lands after their own names.

—Ps. XLIX

The meeting house remembered!
You stood on stilts in the air,
but you fell from your parish.
"All rising is by a winding stair."

—Robert Lowell,
"Jonathan Edwards in Western Massachusetts"

1

THE MEETING HOUSE

Could you believe—here—
in this blank
unstained windowlight?

POSTCARD: BLUESMAN, GLASGOW

With brand name trainers and a thrift store jumper,
A basement bar
And double whisky neat, he plays a number
Whose name I can't remember, tunes his guitar
Then takes another. An opening act for sure
But then I wonder? Now, near ten years spent,
Is he still up there, moaning soulful slow—
Smooth baritone gone gravelly thirty-four,
Whose nine-to-five is just to pay the rent?
Would that. Here's hoping. I can't hear him though.

LABOR DAY

Portland, Maine

After the wedding, before the toasts were over,
because we knew we'd be who-knows-how-long,

we walked all night. Classic New England weather—
hot that day, by then we saw our breath.

Beyond the baseball field, we found a trail
that weaved behind the houses. New-tapped kegs

were hissing, horseshoes clattered, someone yelled.
But further out and up, nothing but treefrogs.

And in that solitude I wished for what
I could stoop down for, grasp, and say, *for this*.

There are fifty-seven working lighthouses in Maine
Which is fewer than you'd think for all that coast.

AMERICAN ROBIN

Hey Sam, I thought you'd like to know
I saw a robin today. The first.
And I remembered how on our last
walk on the coast of the North Sea, you said
the proper robin is small, no bigger
than a golf ball. Ours is a thrush,
a family of songsters second only
to the nightingale. You might know,
I don't. But under a streetlamp
on a rainy Tuesday before work,
before daylight, in time
that's free and unaccounted for, I think I hear it.

CUL-DE-SAC

For days it was the B side to *Veedon Fleece*.
Unflipped it gathered dust. You blew it clean
then set the record spinning, needle-in-groove,
bewildered in the comfort of the thing.

I loved the jacket. The out-of-place-ness of it:
an awkward idyll, faux Edwardian
in its colored-over black and white effect,
familiar and strange on even keel.

I've been there in that leaving, too. I've known
the sting of coming back across my hand,
walked concentric circles of lonely stone
and doubled back, not getting there from here.

BELIEVER'S BAPTISM

Hip deep, you waited in the river,
testified by those who've known you from girlhood.

We waited too, speaking shape-notes over you,
sweet as honey from the lion's skull

or the sound of amazing grace.
But underwater no one could follow you

and you and everyone held their breath.
And just like that the grave was swept away,

the water still trickling like blood down your thigh.

CELLAR SHELF

against the poets

It is what it is—a couple sheets
of plywood, brackets & cement,

two flats of tall boys, a bag of rice,
the glint of pickle jars. A bucket

of carrots packed in sand, an old
pot & a box of nails.

PAINTING OVER THE GROWTH CHART

I had to squint to notice them. The lines
　　that bicker up the door jamb in the kitchen—

a notch for every year, or half-a-year,
　　depending on how much the kids had grown.

A coat of paint is all it takes and if
　　it's not like new, it's good enough for now.

Any sign they ever lived here is blotted out
　　except, perhaps, in Polaroids, stashed

in someone's attic with the bric-a-brac
　　they couldn't bring themselves to throw away—

all crew cuts and towel-capes on summer break
　　circa ninety-nine. But now those kids

are just like me. Beer gut and grays in the drain—
　　fit for this life and mortgaged into it.

JUNIPER,

not evergreen,
its waxen leaves
can handle even

New England weather.
Each is a species
of place, refracted
        as if through green glass
or puddle water.

Here—roots clutch
gravel with all
their courage.

There—the sea air
bottlenecks
like drops of color
on plain paper.

But then again
you ought to know.

for and after Dan Drage

BIRDSEED FOR VERY LUCKY BIRDS

It was all vowel
like the sound of lovers

behind a heavy door—
fricative and labial erased,

plosive evened out,
as senseless as a vow.

It's the tongue of doves
and swallows, the plover

and tit, the pure note
left open and roaming

for scattered seeds and nectar
from open blossoms.

When I am weary of the burden
of meaning, I think of Adam

before he lay with Eve,
yoking sound

to sense, shouldering his other curse
as heavy as the one

that was coming next
and harder to shirk.

ALL SOULS

1957-2017

October is out of breath
as yours left you.

Mine hangs around
like leaves in the branches

of another November.
Birches stretch and fall

like living ghosts.
They rot from the heart

and leave behind
their snowy husks.

So that when I get home
and take off my coat

and hang it in the closet,
I don't mean to speak

of any greater hope
than what I have.

ABRAHAM ON MOUNT MORIAH, TO HIMSELF

Genesis 14

Laughter was his name,
I'll say, when asked

or else I'll simply
wash him away

like so much semen
running down the leg.

I'll take comfort
when it comes and sleep,

even, in sheets
away from this

wanderlust.
Call me Abram.

I'll strike my tent
and go back to Ur.

I'll leave the stars
to count themselves.

LUX IN TENEBRIS

FOR R.S.

Surrounded, half by pavement, half by sea,
I read whatever book it was I had
on hand, by light of streetlamp and strangers' windows.

Could you believe that in a single day
I stood where Patrick Hamilton was burned
and later in the hermit's cave who read

by light of his own illuminated hand?
There is another sort of martyrdom:
to be only text, a lexicon half-shaded

by the reader. Light weighs on everything.
It shines in darkness and it's a dark I've known.
The Word was made flesh and dwelt among us. Yes.

To be a word and never to be read.
If this is hell, it's where I've made my bed.

ORDINARY TIME

The tang of juniper, the dew-wet grass
That grabs your ankles, apples for the taking.
The haze between the hills like smoke at Mass.
   The trees; His stretched arms aching.

The flickering lamps, the fire, the curtains shut.
We'll watch TV, we'll get the biscuits baking.
We sleep like snow that's frozen over but
We're bleary-eyed in waking.

The beer on the table with the week-old fruit.
The shovelful of rain, the lake-ice breaking.
As Advent passes, Christmas follows suit,
   And even love needs making.

II

THE COMMONWEALTH

long distance truck-side
graffiti
reads: *believe the dream*

POSTCARD: GLASGOW NECROPOLIS

What could be more Victorian than this?
A picnic lunch,
The two of us walk the Necropolis
In search of famous dead. You had a hunch
We'd come up empty. Bruce and Burns and Hume,
Of course, were elsewhere, from another age.
Here's where the 19th Century is laid.
Those dark industrial lords have founded tomb
By tomb their city of the dead. Their wage,
Bequeathed to us as romance, fully paid.

ROLLING PIN

Lathe-spun, a scrap of pine
from the woodshop. Sanded, oiled,
dusted with flour from Montreal.
It's waiting at the bake board
beside the pitcher,
beside the mixing bowl.
Its grains course and eddy.
I press the middle
and work along its length's taper.
I scrape the crust off as I go.
It's flawless, despite the knot,
an accident of growth
no workmanship could handle,
black as the eye of a crow,
her tree marked out for timber.

REFLECTION OF A GIRL LOOKING FORLORNLY INTO THE CLOSED BOOKSELLER'S WINDOW, UNKNOWN, C. 2023

Sabbath-shut, impenetrable window glass
condemns what it reflects. Sets, antique
and out-of-print, thin-lipped, scholar-thumbed
fetch a hundred quid on open days.
Behind us, and before, a dry-cleaners, a car,
which frames a frame too dark to make out,
and the girl, off-center and translucent
in British drab stands on ancient pavement.
Eyes inclined and photogenic, she is
an aspect, point-of-view, a saboteur
of grammar, inscrutable and elegant.
And if she looked, it'd be the end of you.

NOSTALGIA

from an old photograph

He cuts a clean, mid-century silhouette
and leans against the late rococo urn
with skinny tie and just-so cigarette.
It's not quite sepia. A slow burn.

Back home, he'll serve his neighbors rye Manhattans.
A couple rounds of bridge complete the scene—
Midwestern, hours behind. Though a photo flattens,
and irons over *if, might-have-been*,

the queuing up, the waiting for the train,
we take them, take them for the real thing.
Vienna, Rome, Madrid, Alsace-Lorraine—
at least it isn't here, the familiar sting,

the ache that comes with coming home. He's seen
the negative, queues up vacation shots
and casts his life against a blank white screen.
Still life with porcelain vase, forget-me-nots.

VARIATIONS ON A FOLK TUNE

I

It's "Bury Me Beneath the Willow Tree"
That melancholy song, an old cassette.
The household dust and everyday debris
Can wait, unlike the morning's cigarette
And coffee, sparrows' daily tête-à-tête,
Unlike the fox who roams to satiate
Her pangs, the tortured saint's not yet, not yet.
Outside, the tree-lined suburbs hesitate,
The oaks and willows on the street don't weep, they wait.

II

Well if I must be buried, I suppose
A willow's not the lowest on my list.
It could be worse. And sure, while I repose,
Some young dumb lovers on a star-crossed tryst
Would knock their hips above me; I'd be pissed—
On more than once by dogs and drunken men.
The roots would rot my—well, you get the gist:
The willow's better than the urn, but then—
Did I say if? Excuse me, what I meant was when.

A PINT OF STILL CIDER

Unfiltered, cellar lain the round of four seasons—
through solstice frost and solstice heat.
And if it rained, who cares?
Still, it's tuber brown,
still cloudy as an April train station,
still the taste of the old year
                            and its windfalls—
Braeburn, Brown Snout, Bramley
from Somerset or Herefordshire.
Still the nose of wild yeast, of cat piss
and meadowsweet.

With the tap turned and the vent eased
the barrel sighs this pungency.

Let it pour.

Everything will stay like it is.
My glass is drained. I call another. I like it like this.

GREENFIELD

(1985-2015)

I was at a loss for once
when they found you like a monk at prayer—
head shorn and pressed against

the driver's side, a decade
of penny-colored bruises
up your arm, the engine

cold. And if I swam
from one side to the other
beneath the overpass

and stuck a folded dollar
on your tongue, still
the bargeman wouldn't come,

he wouldn't bother. Here,
the ground is stiff. We leave
our dead until the thaw.

They burned you, though,
a rosary around your arm.
And when your year's mind came,

they scooped a tablespoon
of ashes and set them in
a wishing lamp, your photo

stapled to the paper.
And as it cleared the trees,
everyone held their breath.

DEATH'S KID BROTHER

If I make my bed in hell, behold, thou art there

Ah, Sleep, have you snuck up on me again?
   Or have this half-drunk wine, my favorite chair
   And wistful thinking caught me unaware?
Don't let me fool you; these lines plucked by my pen
Won't wax immortal. No, the odds are ten
   To one against the dream. My only prayer
   Is to be pinched awake by chilly air
As a dying man would do for dying men.
But if I'm really honest like when rain
   Reveals the rubbish buried under snow,
I'd love for sleep to tear this daisy-chain
   Of days and weeks from stem to stem. But no,
I'm no Endymion. What god will deign
   To leave me be? Not here, nor down below.

SELF-RELIANCE

His sledge was pulled by ox, or so they say,
Till midway through the season, '91.
He even used to tap with wooden taps
And hand-cranked iron drills. His straps and reins,
Antique before the war, were stitched by hand;
He'd wax and mend them every year in May
While listening to the ballgame on his porch.
In years where snow lay just below the belt,
He'd leave the ox at home and shoe his way
Along the trail where once the maples stood.
He'd knock the ice from off the buckets' lids,
Unhook and yoke them, two on either side,
And get them home by dark.
                              Then other years
While tangled in a fog that only March
Could weave, the brimming pails like cataracts,
He'd lead the ox and cart against a wall,
Those veins of stone that course through northern woods.
The drums of sap would slosh with every bump
As, hand-to-rock, he felt his way back home.
His name still hangs above the sugarhouse

But all the gear's been sold or junked as scrap:
The iron kettle, jugs to be refilled,
The snow-shoes, skis, and even nails and bricks.
You might expect the reek of sugar, charred
Into the rafters to remain, but no.
The only thing that's left, besides the sign,
The empties, and a folding metal chair—
A photo of a man, his ox and sledge,
What must have seemed an endless fuel supply
To one who didn't know.
                                    From time to time
His name gets mentioned and, without recourse
To irony, they place it in a list
Of lasts-of-things like *Yankee craftsmanship,*
Resilience,
              self-reliance,
                            dying breeds.

THE VIEW FROM THE
FRENCH KING BRIDGE

If nothing else, the view is lovely—two hills
like arms wrapped around the Connecticut
so high that distance doesn't matter anymore.
The art deco rails are easy enough to climb.
They'll wonder how they built it someday,
when all the little Route 2 towns are empty.
The better question would be why. No one
takes that road to Boston anymore, except
retirees on Sunday drives or skinflints out
to skip the tolls.

                Of them all, just four are said
to have survived. Total deaths unknown.
Even if I'll never have the nerve to stop
the car and walk its length for fear
that passersby would slow, then
think they'd better mind their own business
and drive away, to wherever it is they're headed,
then check the local papers in the morning,
just to see, I'd like to. There, I said it.

SEA CHANTEY

Words lose their thrust where labor is the law.
    I see their leathered fingers clenched around
    The rope, the mop, the gun. Their necks have browned.
The fault-lines slip and crack from cheek to jaw.
They laugh at how their fathers beat them raw
    But never talk about the six who drowned
    In '87. Only two were found,
Each body broken like a lobster claw.

And I'm half-drunk and all my money's spent.
    What can I do but measure out the time
    Like sand? Not words. No, rhythm's hauled the net—
    Old songs my throat won't hazard, can't forget.
    They swell my breath and settle in a rhyme
That lingers in my ear. A testament.

LITTLE HOUSE ON THE PRAIRIE

In light of the fact that Ma's favorite hymn
was called *There is a Happy Land*, you could excuse
the catch in my throat the other night. Even Laura couldn't bring
herself to tell us about the morning Mary woke up blind,
how the light must have filled the room as usual.

It starts, in epic poise, in *medias res*. But then, it's only middle,
like the rest of us. We don't get to see the end. We're left
behind with the dead boy and the burned house in South Dakota.
The story doesn't shut—like a wicket-gate in heavy wind.
No matter how it hits the jamb, it doesn't catch.

THE LOON

Your song is magnetic north.
Feathered wolf. Ghost.

In the deep cuts of the lake,
glacier-made and filled

with snowmelt, you wail and howl
against the sky's vacancy—

that stars are best observed
while lying in the grass

is of no concern to you—
it's all dead fish and gizzard,

depths, the bank's roots.
Hatched among the cracked shells

of less lucky birds,
you hobbled, fledgling, around

the rubbish and made a home.
You drank lake water.

Here, your solitude
is chorus, an echo's echo.

Loon, I have no stone
in the throat, no lyric to grind

the plucked bones of song.
Cover me, then, red-eyed

in midnight's pitch and feathers.
Haunt me again.

THE COMMONWEALTH

Cummington, MA

They burned the house
    and searched the coals for nails.

Now all that's left
    is this foundation stone

storing up the heat
    for when it fails

like the snake who thinks
    the sunlight is his own.

III

HINTERLAND

a sled full of rain
water glazed
with November ice

ALL RISING IS BY A WINDING STAIR

She'd seen his truck around since Monday night,
the beat up '47 Ford outside
the Legion, Tuesday at the barber shop.
And so it came as no surprise when it
pulled up against the curb outside the house.
She'd waited, heard his step in every sound.
And soon enough he climbed the stairs as if
he owned the place, which, she'd pointed out
how many times before, he didn't. It was
her brother's place, the parish priest. He let
them have it on condition that they marry.
And so they did. And had the baby there.
In the very room he slept in now, behind her.
They burned the sheets, bloodied as they were.
It was a miracle they both survived.
That's what the Sisters said, at Christmas, too.
They named him, too, for the Saint of hopeless cases.
She hoped he was asleep, in any case.

"For heaven's sake"—she'd never take God's name
in vain—"don't you know what time it is?"
She opened up the door. She wouldn't bear
to hear his knock, his humble supplication.
"I know," was all he said. He smelled like beer
and cigarettes; no whiskey on his breath.
His denim jacket, his shirt, a week unchanged
all stained with sweat and travel and nicotine.
She knew he'd probably tried to wash the shirt
in some men's room sink along the way.
She paused then let him in without a word.
He took a seat beside the radiator
and rubbed his hands together.
                              "Where've you been?"
she said at last. "Out West. I would've called."
"Your mother told me you were in Quebec
but that was months ago."
                              "I was, a while.
I tried to work it. You know how she is."

She didn't answer but rummaged in her apron,
hanging for the night, and found a pack
of cigarettes and lit one for herself
and one for him.
                    "Is everyone asleep?"
he said after a drag.
                    "As if you care."
"I do. I mean, I want to see them but—"
"But what?"
                "But not like this. I mean it's been too long."
"Do you remember where you were last time?"
"How could I forget?"
                        "I told your son
you were in the hospital, that time,
that's why you had to wear them funny clothes.
I'm glad he's sleeping. *I* don't want to see you."

"I didn't think you would."
                            "Then why're you here?"
He paused then changed his tack. "I have a right."

"I can't see how. We've been apart more time
than not and half those years I wish we were."

"Remember when I'd call you from the road
that year we would have won the Stanley Cup
before I wrecked my ankle. What was that
Nineteen fifty?"
                    "Fifteen years ago.
Is that your argument? Listen, we've been fine.
And if we wanted to we can't go back."
He snubbed his cigarette, got up and paced
and stood a while looking at the jamb
a chart was there. Ages, dates, heights.
"Jude's gotten big. Has he learned to skate?"
"He has. He tried for varsity last year."
"My pair have got to be around here somewhere."
With no response he changed his tack again.
"You know the bridge up Greenfield way?
                                        "Mhm."

"I took a walk last night. Kind of peaceful
I found myself climbing up the rails.
I sat there for a while looking down."
"Leave off. You never could have done it. Sit down."
He sat. "I don't have much."
                              "Whose fault is that?"

"You can be a real bitch sometimes,
you know that? Let me finish. Jesus Christ—"
She crossed herself at that "—I need a favor."
"There's a girl out west." He paused.
                                    "Go on."
"She's pregnant. I'm scared. She isn't doing well.
It's morphine all day long. And when it's not
it's booze. I'm not sure which is worse. It's bad.
She's Indian. I guess she's six months gone."
"You sure it's yours?"
                        "Of course. Well, no. We'll see
When it comes out." He coughed. "If."
"Who turned her on to morphine?"
                                    "That's not the point."
"How old is she?"
                    "That's not the point."
                                            "Then what?
I want to go to bed."
                        The moon peeked through
the curtains, then darkened as a cloud passed over.

"Take it. Please. The baby. If it lives.
Only for a couple months, at least,
I want to see her mother through, and then
if she gets better we'll take her back and live
out West. You'll never hear from us again.
I want to do it right by her this time."
A silence fell that felt like hours. She lit
another cigarette and smoked it halfway down.
"What about your mother, or hers? Why me.
No, not another kid of yours. Never."
"Come on. It's only if it lives. It probably won't.
Ask the priest. Your brother. He'd say you should.
'It's Christian charity.'"

      "Charity starts at home.
Let me heat you up a cup of coffee.
Keep the mug. You have to go. I'm done."
"That's it?"

    "That's it."

      "Fine. I shot my shot.
But first, because you asked. She's just turned twenty.
I'll let you think about it. I'll be in town
another week. Then back where I belong.
I hate it here. It always makes me cold."
"Don't forget your coffee."

      "Thanks. So long."

She leaned against the door and closed her eyes
 and counted thirteen steps, then rushed across
the room and threw the window open wide.
He turned around and she could see his breath.
"Take care of yourself out there. You're a good man.
At least, you aren't a bad one. But don't come back."
"Call me anything but late for supper."

A few months later a telegram arrived:
A single word without a stop: Dead

IV

THE REPUBLIC

no tree in the state
park has seen
the revolution

    and all this time the
    snake was still
    sleeping off his tail

POSTCARD: THE SWANS AT
THE ROYAL BOTANIC GARDENS

'But are they sad?' I overheard her say.
No more than five
Up North with mum for the August bank holiday.
I saw what she meant. They hardly seemed alive
Compared with, overhead, the flock of geese
That flew with everything they had toward France
Or Spain. All of a sudden, all eyes went skyward.
But if the swans were jealous, they held their peace.
I bet they knew, by then, they'd had their chance.
Homesick, maybe. Sad? That wasn't *my* word.

OAR-WORK

Fishing-drunk in the Connecticut
and no miraculous catch, you row for home.

What short thrusts from stern
to bow you give

are given back in long strides across the water.
You leverage the world

which looks to be the thing that's moving
while the boat holds still.

Back and forth you heave the oars
like the sawyer in a cuckoo clock

and it was getting late. And I was afraid
that you would be held there

better than the cleat hitch
you swore would never slip.

ROCKING CHAIR

Come life, Shaker life, come life eternal
shake, shake out of me all that is carnal
—Shaker Hymn

From runged seat to rails
of shingle-split timber
it's woven like the rug it rocks on.

A thick switch of maple
hooked in place becomes
the arm, the brackets at the back.

Varnished with tar, it shines
like borrowed light from a fire
turned against itself,

dim coals collapsing,
going inward, impotent,
a thing so simple and settled-in.

AXE

The axe shaft,
work-hallowed, dull
as newsprint
has forgotten the hickory grove.

Knock off the snow.
Test the edge.

Clutch it

as you would,
if it were offered,
your father's hand.

THE FOOTBRIDGE

after a poem I can no longer find by Edna St. Vincent Millay

Unsafe. Obsolete.
    It's true. I know.
But still, it's sad.
This too, this human feat,
      Must go.

No more will walkers feel
    The space between.
No more will lovers' names, marked in steel,
      Be seen.

This is how it ends:
    We live without it.
And will the river mourn us as it wends?
      I doubt it

ODE

For Bob & Gabriella

Tonight, without sound,
the crocus
unfolds through old snow.

A slow hope: the bloom
like banked coals
holds out till morning.

TO A BIRD

who made her nest inside a statue's palm—
simulacrum of safety, as if a man

would hesitate before he closed his fist
around the straw she plucked from cover-crop,

whose eggs grew cold against the wished-for flesh
and stolen by a boy to throw away;

who didn't know she was herself an image
impressed like sealing wax upon a world

of watchers, weary of the post, on the cusp
like static between one station and another.

DISTILLER

I know enough to know
good spirit. I hear
the warble in the swan neck,

the rhythm of the washback,
the unlooked-for music of oak.
I split and stack and stoke.

I keep time to the chug
of the copper tubing.
I wait the process out.

I hoop together staves
to gather drop by drop
like rain the living water.

BAKER

for Jonathan Stevens

Darkly now the oven
stoked and smoking—smells
adrift—a morning risen

like a hungry ghost. All day
the rasp of plank on stone,
the weight of loaves unzipped

like salmon skin. You stretch
beyond the oven's lip
to reach the deepest loaf.

Nestled in your glove,
you tap the crust for the sound
like someone knocking.

POTTER

She pulls, as though from nothing,
the cup, the pot, a pitcher.
She pinches out the lip—

plain water for the table.
Clay keeps her fingerprints
like glacier lines in granite.

She cranks the wheel by foot,
paints fish on crockery
thistles on coffee cups.

Without a muse, she works
the still point, keeps her clay
for common use.

BESOM

Bound-up straw and whittled birch—
they only ever hung their brooms
to rest on Sunday after church
and sat in sun-swept living rooms.

An heirloom? No. Too commonsense.
Too sturdy, though, to throw away.
And so it's hung here ever since
as if for one long Sabbath-day.

THE BOOKCASE

Here is artifice: these books, this grain—
The knots and notches severed from a pine,
The gilded words on every leather spine,
The lumber scraped and straightened by your plane.
You'd measure twice, cut once, then dull your pain
With work and whisky, sharp as turpentine.
But here is artifice in every line
Unlike the iamb native to the rain.

The clank of power tools becomes a dirge,
As if you're still in the garage, head down
And muttering some short, improper noun.
I'm at my desk still waiting to emerge
with fit words, which don't give up the lie.
Foolish words: *Death, thou shalt die.*

CANADA GEESE

out here our voices don't carry
    but when geese go south
        it sounds like echoes

        of old joy growing older still
          they carry the weather
            from quebec and leave it behind

    with last year's feathers
      they form and scatter
        lucky birds

the same air that froze
    the words to my mouth
      holds them like a breath

POSTCARD: A BAR IN STIRLING

It's breakfast time. A pint goes nicely down
for ten AM.
It's foggy like I like and russet brown.
The bacon, eggs and pudding too, I liked them.
But did it rain that day? I can't decide.
And neither can I say what dress you wore,
Nor yet the joke you told me on the train.
What odds that now as then we're side by side
in bed as barstool asking nothing more?
On second thought, yes thanks, the same again.

ACKNOWLEDGMENTS

Personal thanks to Fr. Ryan Sliwa, Joseph Massey, Claire Roberts, Leah Nielsen, and Don Paterson.

Grateful acknowledgments are made to the editors of the following journals, who first published many of these poems, sometimes in different forms or under different titles.

A number of these poems first appeared in the chapbook, *The Commonwealth (Little Gidding, 2021).*

"Postcard: Bluesman, Glasgow": *FORMA Review*
"Painting Over the Growth Chart": *Poetry Ireland Review*
"Ordinary Time": *First Things*
"Rolling Pin": *Bad Lilies*
"A Pint of Still Cider": *Honest Ulsterman*
"Self-Reliance": *Modern Age*
"Oar-Work": *St. Katherine Review*
"The Commonwealth": *National Review*
"Compline": *Solum*
"Rocking Chair": *Bad Lilies*
"The Footbridge": *Modern Age*
"The Loon": *192 Poetry Magazine*
"Abraham on Mount Moriah, To Himself": *Solum*
"All Souls": *Ekstasis*
"Distiller", "Baker", "Potter": *Banshee*
"Besom": *Ad Fontes*

"The Bookcase": *North American Anglican*
"Postcard: A Bar in Stirling": *Alabama Literary Review*
"To a Bird": *Ekstasis*
"Cul-de-Sac": *Dappled Things*
"Lux in Tenebris": *Dappled Things*

ABOUT THE AUTHOR

Dan Rattelle earned his MFA at the University of St Andrews, but other than his too-brief stay there he is a lifelong resident of Western Massachusetts and has no plans to leave. *Painting Over the Growth Chart* is his first full-length poetry collection and is a version of his MFA Thesis, *The Meetinghouse*. He currently manages two cemeteries in his hometown.